Things I Want To Remember Not To Forget

CHRIS WADDELL

ISBN: 978-0-9975910-0-2

Printed in China.

For all of us who want to remember

Acknowledgements

Thank you to Lisa Antonucci and Dana Craig for your gentle and thorough editing. You gave me confidence in the project. Sandra More, I appreciate your exhaustive read of the first draft. You helped me find the right path. Nomi Bergman, this book wouldn't have started without you. Thank you for the idea to write it and your belief in me. To my wife Jean, my mother Nancy, my buddy John and my assistant Rachel, thank you for reading everything I wrote, but more importantly, for your support of me throughout.

Drawing by Chris Waddell
To accompany **Chapter 9 Try Something New**

Contents

CHAPTER 1: Commencement   1

CHAPTER 2: It's Not What Happens to You. It's   7
What You Do with What Happens to You.

CHAPTER 3: Be Cocky   11

CHAPTER 4: Say Yes More Often   15

CHAPTER 5: Something Small Can Lead   19
to Something Big

CHAPTER 6: Celebrate the Victories and Defeats   23
Along the Way

CHAPTER 7: The Pebble in My Shoe Affects Me More   27
Than the Boulder in My Path

CHAPTER 8: Just Because Everyone Does It,   31
Doesn't Make It Any Less Spectacular

CHAPTER 9: Have a Strategy   35

CHAPTER 10: Try Something New   39

CHAPTER 11: Final Thought   43

Things I Want to Remember Not to Forget

Commencement

When the president of Middlebury College asked me to be the 2011 commencement speaker, I thought of a Dalai Lama quote: "Remember that not getting what you want is sometimes a wonderful stroke of luck."

Breaking my back as a freshman ski racer in 1988 led me to become one of the best Paralympians in history. After retiring from competitive sport, attempting to change the world by handcycling unassisted to the summit of Mt. Kilimanjaro in Africa left me feeling like a failure when I had to be carried for one hundred feet over a boulder field just below the crater rim. That so-called failure freed me of the belief held since the accident that I had to be a superhero in order to be equal. Not getting what you want can be a wonderful stroke of luck.

But ski racing was my first love and greatest teacher. It ripped out my heart and forced me to put it back in. At six years old, I'd started skiing on the man-made snow at tiny Mt. Tom, just ten minutes from our house and an hour and a half west of Boston. My parents were ski instructors. They would pick up my brother and me from school and bring us to the mountain. Each run, I tried to impress Rob Broadfoot, my very cool coach, and each run he would tell me what I did well and what I could do better. By thirteen, I was the best in the region. By fifteen, I was ready to walk away. Not only hadn't I won a race in a year and a half, I hadn't even reached the finish line. Quitting seemed the only escape from the pile of despair that grew with each failure, but I knew if I walked away from that fight it would be easier to walk away from the next one.

At Middlebury, I set the goal to be an All-American. There were only twenty per year, and there were at least a hundred if not two hundred ahead of me, but if everything went exactly right, it could happen. I prepared for that moment. Each day throughout the summer and fall, I pushed myself beyond the point that I wanted to quit. Each time I resisted the temptation, I readied myself for the most important starting gate of my life. But as it turned

2

out, I never got that chance. On the first day of Christmas vacation, my binding popped off in the middle of a turn. I broke two vertebrae, paralyzing myself from the waist down.

After surgery and two months recovery, I left the hospital on a Friday and returned to school, amidst surprise and support, two days later. At the final race, held at the Middlebury Snow Bowl the following weekend, I reconnected with the ski world, watching in my wheelchair from the bottom. The next season, my coach kept me on the team, and the father of a teammate bought my first monoski. Three hundred and sixty-two days after the accident, I skied again, though I didn't make one turn that first day. Following a week of falls, I could go from the top without falling.

At my first race, totally unprepared and scared to death, I morphed back into a ski racer in the way that I carried and saw myself, which led me to win more Paralympic medals – twelve – than any male monoskier in history. Also a wheelchair racer, I won a silver medal in the 200 meters at the 2000 Summer Paralympic Games in Sydney, Australia. I was one of the few to win World Championships in both the winter and summer, yet more than winning, I felt a responsibility to stretch the imagination of the general public with every race. I wanted them to see people like me for our potential and not what we had lost, which was also what prompted me to attempt Kilimanjaro.

Skiing taught me who I was and who I could be. I won, I failed, I got hurt, I got up, I improved, I failed again, I kept going, I faced my fears, I succumbed to my fears, I laughed, I cried, and I gathered experiences. It was my first love and my window into myself, but after my accident it became my life. Getting back on the slopes represented recovery. When I took all that my fear hurled at me, turned it around and shaped it as power, I felt like I'd succeeded not just as a skier, but as a person.

Commencements are glorious moments when an ending and a beginning occupy the same space. In our non-stop lives, they represent an opportunity to pause, to assess the past, and to plan for the future. Amidst the reflection, celebration, and optimism lay the landmarks, if we can recognize them. On graduation day, the academic leaders collected outside Middlebury's iconic Old Chapel in robes, caps, and medallions signifying their academic distinction and looking like a scene from *Harry Potter.* My new blue-and-white hood, for Honorary Doctorate in Humane Letters, gained me entry, but I worried that the enormity of the day would render me mute on the stage. A bog of mud – the result of the spring rains that I remembered so well from my time as a student – hid just below the glorious blue-sky, green-grass day, and clumped on my wheels.

When fear had threatened me at the start of a ski race, I'd simplify my approach. Just be fast and confident to the first gate. When I did it, the nerves subsided, and I wanted to go faster. Employing the same technique, I said, "I've heard a lot of graduation speeches. If there is one common theme it's that I don't remember anything from any of them, so here's my message: It's not what happens to you. It's what you do with what happens to you. Now you can go back to sleep, because I know that many of you didn't make it to bed last night."

Like life, ski racing is a constant cycle of learning, forgetting, and relearning. Just because I knew something for one race didn't mean that I'd remember it for the next. This short book combines lessons from ski racing, as well as anecdotes, thoughts, tricks, hooks, and perspectives from my reflection for that graduation speech. I call it ***Things I Want to Remember Not to Forget*** because it's so easy to forget. Before each ski race, I ingrained the technique by making really big turns on really flat trail. To stay upright, each move had to be perfect. Speed wouldn't prop me up. Slowing down allowed me to find my center. I hope that this book allows you to slow down, return to center, and remember what you don't want to forget.

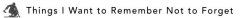 Things I Want to Remember Not to Forget

It's Not
What Happens to You.
It's What You Do
With What Happens to You.

On my way home from the airport following a two-week trip to the other side of the world, I parked my car in front of the mailboxes at the end of my street and started to pull my chair out and attach the wheels. As I did, a girl who was about six years old rode up on her little pink bike with pink streamers flowing from the handlebars. She asked, "What happened to your legs?" I was tired from the travel and didn't particularly want to have a conversation with a six year old, but I also felt a responsibility to answer her question, because as a member of the disabled community, I often feel invisible. From the time we're very young, we're taught not to stare at someone who looks different. If we don't get a chance to stare and ask questions, we'll never see someone who looks different from us. So I answered the little girl's question as best I could.

I told her that I was a ski racer in college. My first day of Christmas vacation, my brother and I met a few buddies at the mountain where we'd grown up and took a couple of runs before training. In the middle of a turn my ski popped off. I fell in the middle of the trail, didn't hit anything but the ground, and broke two vertebrae.

I tried to describe what happened to me in terms that she could understand. I asked her, "You know those bumps on your back? Well those are bones, and those bones protect the nerves, and the nerves carry messages from your brain to the rest of your body. If you want your arm to move, your brain sends a message along those nerves to the muscles in your arm, and your arm moves. Breaking those bones damaged the spinal cord. It was like cutting a power cord. The message can't go from my brain to my legs or from my legs back to my brain. I can't feel my legs and I can't move them."

"So you'll never walk again."

"No, probably not."

As she rode away, she said, "Well, that's too bad."

I wish that I'd stopped her. I wish that I had told her that it wasn't too bad. If I'd never had my accident, I never would have been the best in the world at anything, and I had been the best monoskier in the world. She just saw what happened to me. She didn't see what I did with what happened to me.

I want to remember not to forget that it's not what happens to me. It's what I do with what happens to me.

Things I Want to Remember Not to Forget

10

Be Cocky

Even before I'd learned to monoski, even when all the monoskiers beat me, I knew that I would be best in the world because I had an unfair advantage. Unlike the others, I knew the feeling of making a good turn because I'd been a ski racer. Perhaps I was bragging when I said I would be the best, but I was being cocky. Cocky was the belief that I possessed something that no one else did, and I believed it without question. That was my advantage. It allowed me to welcome fear, worry, and uncertainty into the start because it made me their master. Defeats and failures became necessary steps to the inevitable goal.

When I started to monoski, my conviction was so profound

that I didn't recognize myself, but I liked it. I'd never believed in myself like that. Part had to be my ski-racing knowledge, but part was far more personal. Skiing represented my recovery from the accident. Each time I pushed into the starting gate, I had to confirm that I was whole and successful and that I wouldn't return to my fearful self. Each time I rose to the occasion I became cockier.

Years after I had retired, I pushed into another starting gate of sorts: an open mic night at a comedy club. Now, I make my living as a speaker. If I could be funny I'd get hired more. By the time I found parking and the right floor for the club amongst the Lulu Lemons and Restoration Hardwares, a long line had formed. That's when I remembered that I had neglected to bring support. Instinct told me to turn around before they learned that I was there to try to be funny. It implored me to leave again when one of the guys said that my end of the line probably wouldn't make it in, but I stayed, even though I felt like the new kid in school.

This wasn't my first time to open mic. I'd done it four or five times over twenty years, but this time, I wanted to tell jokes and stories about being in a wheelchair. I had my three-minute set down, but when the spotlight shone in my eyes, I couldn't deliver my line. Unlike the ski race, I couldn't commit to the first turn or the first line. I froze. The voice in my head said, "You know they expect you to say something, right?" I answered that, yes, I knew they expected me to say something, but nothing came. By the time I finally found words, I breezed through my set so quickly that I didn't give them a chance to laugh.

Driving home, I could barely keep my eyes open. The nerves had exhausted me. I hadn't given myself a chance. I wondered what I would have risked if I had been cocky. They might have thought that I wasn't funny. I could live with that. The experience wouldn't kill me, but if I kept running away, I'd die a little bit each time I didn't let myself try. Each time my conviction wanes, I look at the Teddy Roosevelt quote on my wall:

> "*It is not the critic who counts, not the man who points out how the strong man stumbles, or how the doer of deeds could have done them better. The credit belongs to the man who is actually in the arena, whose face is marred by dust and sweat and blood; who strives valiantly; who errs, who comes up short again and again, for there is no effort without error or shortcoming; but who knows the great enthusiasms, the great devotions; who spends himself for a worthy cause. Who at best knows in the end the triumph of high achievement, and who at the worst, if he fails, fails while daring greatly so that his place shall never be among those cold and timid souls who know neither victory nor defeat.*"

But cocky doesn't just happen. One time in class, I had returned to acting after retirement (more about that in the next story), a fellow student asked the teacher, "What if I just can't get over the nervousness of auditioning?" He responded, "Just be confident," to titters of laughter from those of us relieved that his propensity to be flip hadn't been aimed at us. He followed with, "You're an actor, right? Act confident when you get up in the morning, when you brush your teeth. When you get into your car. When you get out of your car. Before you know it, you'll be confident."

The next time I go to open-mic night, I'm going to put Post-it® notes all over the house that say, "You're funny!!" and "Be cocky!!" Then at least when I give my performance I'll know that I'd given the best one that I could give in that moment. If it's not good enough, I'll just have to figure out how to make it better next time.

I want to remember to be cocky so that I never become a cold and timid soul.

Say Yes More Often

When I broke my back on December 20, 1988, I thought the only way to recover was to walk. After all, when I got a cold, I'd rest, drink lots fluids, and maybe take some medication. Eventually, I wouldn't have a cold anymore. My situation had to be the same. Things had to return to the way that they'd been before the accident, but no surgeries, treatments, or magic pills could cure paralysis. My parents and I explored programs that helped paraplegics walk by attaching electrodes to the leg muscles, as well as ones searching for a cure, before settling on Shake-A-Leg, a holistic healing center based in Portsmouth, Rhode Island.

I'm rolling in here, but I'm walking out, I thought. Instead of labs, Shake-A-Leg had rooms in a former nunnery for massage, Rolfing, Feldenkrais, body movement, physical therapy, weight training, nutrition, and psychology. Since modern medicine didn't have an answer for me, my recovery would hinge on my ability to source my greatest strength. Finding it would mean exploring depths I'd never explored.

Despite a lifetime of never quite feeling good enough or smart enough, I'd always believed that greatness lay within me if I could access it. In the summer of 1989, six months after my accident, I didn't have a choice. To achieve the impossible, I would need all my strength and then some. Saying yes to new opportunities, possibilities and ideas was the only way that I could realize previously undiscovered strength.

I'd never had a massage before arriving at Shake-A-Leg, never had the deep tissue work of Rolfing to break existing patterns, or the proprioception self-awareness of Feldenkrais to teach new patterns of movement and possibly find alternate ways to move my legs. Instead of pooh-poohing the new-age therapy, I embraced it. When the therapist asked me to breathe into a spot on my back, I breathed into it with all I had. I freed my mind and body from the shackles of conventional belief. In the traditional therapies, I pushed my body to and beyond its limits. When a weight trainer, a cube of muscle at five-foot-ten and about two hundred and ten pounds, asked me what my goals were, I told him I didn't care what he did to me, I just wanted to get better. When the physical therapist strapped plastic Pillo Polo® mallets to my legs with ace bandages and athletic tape, I tried to walk between the parallel bars.

My goal was to walk on straight-leg braces fifty percent of the time like Harry Horgan, Shake-A-Leg's founder. Harry used braces and crutches when he went to the movies or to a restaurant. He had stood at full height when he got married.

Near the end of the summer, my braces finally arrived at the same time as Manhattan Class Company, an off-off Broadway Theater Company. Bernie Telsey, who partnered in the company with Bobby LuPone, asked if I would audition for the play. I told him that I was an athlete and didn't do that kind of stuff, plus I had been waiting all summer to walk. He persisted. I auditioned. After all, I'd said yes to everything that summer. To my surprise, they cast me as the lead.

The play stretched me more than any of the therapies because it forced me to confront my desire to run away. In eighth grade I had presented an award at my school's Winter Sports Banquet. When my moment came, I'd totally forgotten what I was supposed to say. My voiced cracked and quivered and my knees shook. I practically said, "Here," to the recipient. At rehearsals, Bernie and Bobby made me do improv and scenes in gibberish. Against every instinct of self-preservation, I'd jumped into the abyss of potential embarrassment.

On opening night, five hundred people filed into the middle-school auditorium. I peaked around the curtain, summoning the nerves for my final test. In that moment, I realized that I was performing again. Waiting for the curtain was like being at the start of a ski race. I had to accept the rush of nerves and control them, so that I could play. The audience intoxicated me. Bernie and Bobby brought me to an unexplored place. By forcing me to face my fears, they'd shown me that I could achieve the impossible.

At the start of the summer, I'd thought I would be whole if I could stand to look people in the eye. At the end, being whole had nothing to do with walking or standing. Whole was happiness, health, having dreams, and being willing to jump into the abyss. Saying yes opened my eyes and my heart to unexplored possibilities that revealed the unrealized power for which I'd been searching.

I want to remember not to forget to say yes when fear and insecurity tempt me to say no. I want to remember to say yes because that's the path to my greatest power.

Something Small
Can Lead to Something Big

I don't know about you, but big goals frustrate me if they seem out of reach. When I decided to handcycle to the top of Mt. Kilimanjaro, I wanted to change the world. If I, a wheelchair user, could make it to the top under my own power, then I could turn the world's perception of disability upside down by shifting focus from less and limited, to dreams and creativity. I hoped to bring people together by showing my struggles in a documentary film because no matter who we are, we struggle. Those who have had to persevere just have more stories to tell and lessons to teach.

But, in order to affect any change, I had to make it to the top of the mountain. The trip from the 6,000-foot base to the 19,340-foot summit would involve 13,340 feet of climbing and more than 40 miles of handcycling starting in a rainforest, finishing on a glacier, and traveling through five climate zones. The cone at the top of the long-dormant volcano with its steep slope and loose terrain would present the greatest challenge. My rear wheels might just dig a hole in the gravelly scree. To make matters worse, I was a sprinter not an endurance athlete. As a ski racer and wheelchair sprinter, the vast majority of my races hadn't lasted longer than two minutes, and I was asking myself to pedal nine to ten hours a day for five to twelve days. I didn't mind hurting, sometimes to the point that my hair and teeth hurt, but I needed to know that I could stop, allowing the pain to subside. On the mountain, there was no finish line other than reaching the top and returning to the bottom. I could stop whenever I wanted, just as long as I started again.

With the idea of stretching me to an endurance athlete, my guide Dave Penney and I started a callusing process, toughening me up by going longer and further and then repeating it the next day. My first big climb was a seven-hour slog up Crested Butte Mountain Resort. On a paved bike path at the end, I could see Dave's house about a mile away. I briefly contemplated pedaling hard to break what was a delicate drive train at the time before resigning myself to grind my way to the finish. That night, I was barely strong enough to lift myself out of the shower. Then we did it again the next day.

Another time on the White Rim Trail in Moab, Utah, I labored five hours back and forth over Hardscrabble Hill and through the deepest sand, measuring my energy to the finish line, which was Dave's truck, only to have him say, "I'll pick you up five miles down the road." Grudgingly, I kept going when I felt positive that I had to stop. On 14,271-foot Mt. Evans in Colorado, I wanted to throw a temper tantrum like a little kid. Each turn appeared to be the final one only to dash my hopes when it turned out to be a false summit. I resigned that if I threw the tantrum, I'd just have to pick myself up and keep going, so I never threw the fit, but finally made the summit.

My biggest test was three days in the Utah desert when I completed the 105-mile White Rim Trail. The last day was the hottest. With just twelve miles to go, I was so sure I'd vomit that I called the camera crew so they could capture the scene. I didn't get sick, but did struggle to finish as darkness fell.

In advance of the climb, a member of my team did some math, estimating that it would take me 528,000 pedal revolutions to make the summit of Kilimanjaro. That sounded like a lot of little things to achieve something big, but as a ski racer I knew the real work happened when it didn't look like there was any progress.

I'd always thought my breakthroughs were like my eighth-grade science experiment. My classmates and I put ice in a beaker over a lit Bunsen burner then took the temperature every minute. The temperature graph went up consistently, flattened out, went up again, and flattened a second time. When the temperature was flat, the energy had transformed the solid to liquid and then the liquid to gas. In skiing, I would work day after day with no change, but then, like the temperature, my results would go up. When I become frustrated by my big goals, I think of that ice block's amazing transformation and the latent heat that made it happen. I'll never know exactly how many revolutions it took me to reach the summit, but I know that a lot of little things eventually result in a big one.

I want to remember, especially when I'm frustrated, not to forget that every big thing is the product of a whole lot of little ones.

Celebrate the Victories and Defeats Along the Way

In third grade, our teacher asked us to write a story. Mine, about a family of rabbits, was by far the most elaborate with a collection of characters, multiple chapters, and page after page of story. After I read it to the class, my teacher flattered me, saying that it was worthy of publishing, though it never was. In time, however, my desire to tell stories became a hidden dream. My English papers, bloody with red ink, convinced me that I just wasn't very good. Years passed yet I harbored dreams of telling stories. Finally, with John, one of my best friends, I started a writing group. We both wanted to write, and we needed support and help, especially getting out of our own way.

When I started skiing, Rob Broadfoot had guided my daily progress. But as an adult wanting to tell stories, one voice in my head expected to be good immediately. The other echoed a bumper sticker I'd once seen, "It's better to be thought an idiot than to open your mouth and remove all doubt." So I produced nothing. Knowing that we had to manage expectations, learn, and ease our fears, John and I wrote bylaws for our group. Most prominent among them, we had to celebrate the minor victories like writing a query letter to an agent, contacting an editor, or finishing a rough draft.

Blogs became my first foray as I told the story of our Kilimanjaro climb. Still, I agonized with my finger over the "publish" button, seeing all those bloody teachers' comments, convinced that I would remove all doubt. To my surprise, people liked my stories and perspective. Celebrating those minor victories allowed my fragile ego to make the first step.

Minor victories are important, but defeats contain more learning. Preparing for the Kilimanjaro climb, we did a scouting trip in June 2008. Scouting or not, I thought, let's go for the top now. Then it took me four days to get to the second camp. One of our cameramen kept saying, "It's five minutes up the trail." Those five minutes took me hours. Each time I finished a tough section I figured the going would get easier, but the old saying, "What goes up must come down," was broken. What went up, kept going up. I couldn't even see the top of the mountain when our guides told me that if the team and porters didn't push and pull me, I wouldn't get a chance to see it. The trip would be a failure. Feeling defeated, I swallowed my pride as the cameras captured me riding on others' strength.

That trip, I made it to the Hans Meyer Cave at almost 17,000 feet. They let me pedal on the cone above Kibo Hut to experience the steep, loose scree. I didn't see the summit, but I learned the mountain. Making it to the top would require long days of high rpms instead of pure strength because my heart and lungs could recover while my muscles, once exhausted, couldn't. The handcycle needed to be narrower to better fit on the trail. The back wheels had to be moved under my hips to improve traction and efficiency. The lessons I learned from that scouting trip insured my success a little more than a year later.

I want to remember not to forget to celebrate the victories and defeats along the way because they represent the encouragement and lessons that eventually lead to success.

 Things I Want to Remember Not to Forget

The Pebble in My Shoe Affects Me More Than the Boulder in My Path

When I broke my back, I couldn't get out of the hospital bed by myself. I couldn't dress myself. I went from one hundred and seventy-five pounds down to one hundred and twenty-five pounds. My leg muscles melted away. I couldn't walk and had lost many prospects for my future. Yet, it was the most powerful that I've ever been because my life achieved a simplicity that I'd never experienced. I let go of frustration, worry, and insecurity, which had blocked my way so many times, and which now I could not allow to prevent my recovery. Each day, I had to get better even if it was only a little bit. One little thing led to another and another, building momentum. Two months after the accident, I was ready to return to college when the head doctor called me into his office.

From behind his mahogany desk, in a white smock, white shirt, and subtle tie, he said, "You're not ready to leave." A crushing blow since that's all I wanted. My fly sat over my left hip. I still hadn't mastered getting dressed in bed with legs that were like wet noodles. The balance of power favored him, yet I asked, "Why am I not ready to leave?" He said, "Because you haven't been depressed."

That perplexed me. I had feared that depression would prevent me from moving forward, confirming a life of limitations. Don't get me wrong, I knew that I was paralyzed, but I couldn't handle that my life and dreams might be over at age twenty. He saw me as a ticking time bomb, figuring that eventually I'd see the depth of the situation. He worried that when I did, I'd be really depressed.

It took seventeen years – until my thirty-sixth birthday – which also happened to be the Closing Ceremony for the 2004 Summer Paralympics in Athens, Greece, my seventh and final Games, for me to experience that kind of depression. Winning had made me remarkable in the way that I'd always craved. It had also kept me from confronting many issues of being in a wheelchair. But in retirement, seemingly with the ability to do whatever I wanted, I questioned my identity, my purpose, my ability to contribute, and I feared I would never be remarkable again.

Each morning, I didn't know where to start or what to do. Frustration, worry, and insecurity formed the pebbles in my shoes while past success provided a comfortable crutch for my ego. Deadlines slipped from days to weeks to years. I sold art in a gallery for a while, represented some Paralympic athletes as an agent, and secretly tried to teach myself to write, but didn't move forward. Lack of progress haunted me. Each time I woke, my heart pounded like a horse galloping around a corner on wet tile.

Discipline and hard work had made me successful. I missed waking early to do yoga before training, going straight to the gym from the mountain – one more set, one more rep – teaching my body to react by executing perfectly in training. I missed dedicating myself. The realization that I needed a goal bigger than myself represented the first step in my recovery. As an athlete, winning had been important, but pushing disabled sport and the image of disabled people had been my higher purpose. Climbing Kilimanjaro renewed that purpose and reengaged my passion. I worked harder when I didn't want to let people down. My passion and discipline began to work for me again.

I want to remember not to forget that the boulders in my path help me overcome the pebbles in my shoe.

 Things I Want to Remember Not to Forget

30

Just Because Everyone Does It, Doesn't Make It Any Less Spectacular

Almost everyone learns to walk, speak, and read, but think for a moment just how spectacular those things are. They indicate amazing potential, don't they? We all went from this lump of baby to rolling over, crawling, walking, and running. Could you imagine trying that now? We'd be so frustrated by the end of the first day that we'd never attempt it again. We'd just lie on that floor. Have you tried to learn a foreign language? Memorization, flash cards, grammar rules … But as toddlers we learned noises that became words both spoken and written. Isn't it amazing that we all learned such transformational and intricate things? When big dreams overwhelm me, I remember what I learned before I knew what I was doing. Isn't that an indication of great potential? Maybe thinking is the problem.

My niece is now a teenager, but I remember when she pulled herself up to standing, tottered, fell, and repeated the process over and over. Her head was too big for her body then. Her belly protruded. The diaper counterbalanced the belly to a certain extent, but the weak link was her tiny feet. Grossly inadequate for the job of keeping the body upright, she flexed and flexed them. She fell and got back up. I doubt she considers learning to walk these days, but she should. She went from zero to unlimited potential.

Speaking, reading, and writing are equally impressive. We learned sounds, symbols that represent sounds, to combine symbols creating words, sentences, paragraphs, thoughts, concepts, and opinions. How amazing is it that we can communicate, learn, and educate? Speaking, reading, and writing give us the building blocks to comprehend everything, but we don't consider the significance because someone is always smarter or more accomplished. Yet, with time we can learn whatever we want.

Time and patience might be the key. My niece never quit. Once she could pull herself up to standing, she didn't take a break. She didn't give up. She just kept plugging away. There has to be a message there. So much of learning is just plugging away, but at least we know that we've achieved incredible things already. If we've done it once, we can do it again.

I want to remember not to forget that I've already achieved the impossible, so why not try again?

 Things I Want to Remember Not to Forget

Have a Strategy

As a kid I suffered from asthma. "It's all in your head," my father said. "It's psychosomatic." His words frustrated me. I just wanted to get air into my lungs. My nose and throat felt like they'd grown together. The more I strained, the less air wheezed in. My muscles squeezed my ribs like a boa constrictor. The more I tried not to think about asthma restricting my breathing, the more I thought about it. By some strange psychosomatic amnesia, I outgrew asthma when I broke my back. Call it trading one affliction for another, but I didn't have any trouble breathing until weeks before the Kilimanjaro climb.

My final physical test was the Off-Road Handcycle

World Championships in Crested Butte, Colorado. Kilimanjaro wasn't a race, but I was slower than the hikers. To make it to camp in daylight I had to be fast, especially since I'd taken twice as long to reach camp on the scouting trip. I needed to win this race to prove that I could keep up in Africa. Starting at 9,115 feet, the hill climb was the first event. Even though I'd trained for long pedaling days, I'd chosen the one-hour hill sprint as my barometer. Suffering through as much pain as I could tolerate, I broke the existing record by ten minutes and won by one minute, confirming my preparation.

The next morning I woke feeling like I had a rug burn on my throat and lungs. For the first time in years, I couldn't breathe. I attempted to smooth my self-conscious swallows and banish all thought, but the more I tried not to think, the more I thought, and the more difficult breathing became. Air usually rushed in and out when I climbed. That day it didn't move at all. The results didn't matter. I had a new problem. My lungs might fail me on the mountain. All of our work might be wasted by my psychosomatic weakness.

At home, I sought my yoga teacher. Lying on my living room floor, I followed her instructions to wring all the air from my lungs and then wait. Stomach flexed, I waited, then a glorious inhale sparked without command. Cool, rushing air soothed my nostrils as muscles bellowed my lungs full.

I had my strategy: Don't strain to inhale; exhale with the confidence that my lungs would fill on their own. My fears of asphyxiation never materialized on the mountain. When I felt stressed, I exhaled.

I want to remember not to forget that I need strategies to combat my fears.

 Things I Want to Remember Not to Forget

Try Something New

"Who is that?" my elementary school music teacher said. Fear sat me up straight. That prickly feeling played at my stomach. "Chris Waddell, is that you? Why are you intentionally trying to ruin my song?" That's when I learned I couldn't sing. Nothing intentional. I was just singing, something I never did again in public. Mouthing the words, I made peace that there were some things I couldn't do. Apparently, I couldn't sing. I couldn't draw either. Some people could make a song beautiful, and some could transfer a scene from their eye to the paper. In third grade, I learned that I was not one of those people.

Then this fall I had lunch with a friend at a dumpling

place in New York City's Chinatown. He fit our meal between karate class and ballroom dancing, explaining that he never learned a sense of kinesthetic awareness as a kid, and he wanted to know it now. During the meal, he also explained he had studied cooking so that he would have at least one dinner to entertain guests. I was in the midst of a two-month tour of school presentations for my foundation, and had been talking to a publisher about my children's book on the Kilimanjaro climb.

Back in 2009, after I had come off Kilimanjaro, my mother had told me I should write a children's book on the climb. I couldn't have been more exhausted. Travel and speaking had occupied every moment of the last two months. Even though I loved children's books and loved the idea of producing one even more, I couldn't imagine finding the emotional space to write until I broke my leg scooting down my basement stairs to train on my stationery bike. Lying on my bed with my leg raised over my heart, inspiration hit me. I grabbed a pen and computer paper and wrote and drew as fast as I could, hoping I'd finish before I lost the thread. One book quickly became four, but they just sat in a folder in my office. My drawings were just stick-figure placeholders. The publisher had hired an illustrator, who was great, but I wanted to write and draw.

When I returned home from my two months of

presentations, I found a book called ***Drawing on the Right Side of the Brain,*** by Betty Edwards. A friend had loaned it to me more than twenty years prior. The binding glue had turned to dust, but I was determined to follow the exercises all the way to the end. While I'd thought singing and drawing were God-given talents, Ms. Edwards wrote that if you had enough dexterity to write your name, you could draw. The key was to see properly. Optimistic yet skeptical, I followed the exercises every day. To my surprise, my images started to take shape like solving a puzzle or an archeological dig. Recently, I took the inspiration of an idea, "Is it lonely to be a four-leaf clover?", and turned it into a children's story with colored drawings for my wife's birthday. It was the first one I'd completed, and it was the product of trying something new.

The exhilaration of learning to draw bent the shape of my view of myself. I'd thought people either could or couldn't sing or draw, but now I'm not so sure. Maybe I won't try to sing, since my singing is kind of like halitosis, but I could learn to play guitar or speak Italian. Each time I learn something new it spurs me to try something else.

I want to remember not to forget to try something new because that's the way to get to do what I want. Learning is cool.

Final Thought

If there is anything to take from a graduation speech, it's that everyday should be a graduation. Everyday should be an opportunity to stop, just for a moment, and look forwards and backwards. Otherwise, one day spills into the next. One day becomes ten or twenty years. When I retired from competitive sport I missed the portal that was the start of a ski race. Months in advance I'd prepare for that definitive moment. I missed it because of the shape it had given to my days and progress and the hope of what I might find on the other side.

These days, speaking replaces that performance portal, but it falls short. Speaking is not as fluid as the start of a